Mick Manning grew up in Haworth, West Yorkshire and studied
Illustration at the Royal College of Art in London.
Brita Granström grew up on a farm in Sweden and studied
Illustration at Konstfack in Stockholm.
Their distinctive books have won many awards. Their first book,
The World is Full of Babies, won the Smarties Silver Prize. Mick and Brita
have four sons and live in the north east of England. Their other books
with Frances Lincoln include the critically acclaimed Fly on the Wall series:
Roman Fort, Pharaoh's Egypt, Viking Longship and *Greek Hero*. Both *Roman Fort*
Viking Longship were shortlisted for the English Association 4-11 Awards.
Snap! is the follow-up to *Yuck!* which was a regional winner of the
Highland Book Awards 2006.

snap!

Mick Manning

Brita Granström

F

FRANCES LINCOLN
CHILDREN'S BOOKS

Look!

A fly buzzing by...

Fly is
in Frog's belly!

Frog gobbled
the fly that came
buzzing by...

Snap!

Frog is in Duckling's belly!

Duckling guzzled
the frog that gobbled
the fly that came
buzzing by...

Duckling is in Pike's belly!

Pike ate the duckling that guzzled the frog that gobbled the fly that came buzzing by...

Pike is in Fisherman's belly!

Fisherman caught the pike that ate the duckling that guzzled the frog that gobbled the fly that came buzzing by...

Here snores the bear that swallowed the fisherman that caught the pike that ate the duckling

that guzzled the **frog**
that gobbled the **fly** that came buzzing by...

Look!

Another fly buzzing by...

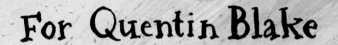

For Quentin Blake

First published in Great Britain and the USA in 2006 by
Frances Lincoln Children's Books, 4 Torriano Mews,
Torriano Avenue, London NW5 2RZ
www.franceslincoln.com

First paperback edition 2008

British Library Cataloguing in Publication Data available on request

ISBN 978-1-84507-611-5

Illustrated with collage, coloured paper and black ink.

Printed in China

9 8 7 6 5 4 3 2 1

MORE TITLES FROM
FRANCES LINCOLN CHILDREN'S BOOKS

Yuck!
Mick Manning and Brita Granström

What's for supper?
A wriggly worm? YUCK!
Come and join all sorts of babies in the slimiest, stinkiest,
most revolting feast ever. But with spiders, lizards and rotten eggs
on the menu, who will say YUM! and who will say YUCK!

ISBN 978-1-84507-423-4

Dino-Dinners
Mick Manning and Brita Granström

When dinosaurs get hungry, who eats what – and who eats who?
How do we know what dinosaurs ate?
Who liked meat and who liked veg?
Who munched anything they could find?
Discover exactly who or what is on the menu when it's dino-dinnertime!

ISBN 978-1-84507-689-4

Everybody Poos
Taro Gomi

Let's talk about POO!
Some animals poo on land, some poo in the water.
Some stop to poo. Others do it on the move.
I poo and you poo too. Every living thing has to eat, and so everybody poos!

ISBN 978-1-84507-258-2

Frances Lincoln titles are available from all good bookshops.
You can also buy books and find out more about your favourite titles,
authors and illustrators on our website: www.franceslincoln.com